INFORMATION
EXPLORER
JUNIOR

# Find the Facts with Encyclopedias

by Ann Truesdell

CHERRY LAKE PUBLISHING · ANN ARBOR, MICHIGAN

A NOTE TO PARENTS AND TEACHERS: Please remind your children how to stay safe online before they do the activities in this book.

CHERRY LAKE
Publishing

A NOTE TO KIDS: Always remember your safety comes first!

Published in the United States of America
by Cherry Lake Publishing
Ann Arbor, Michigan
www.cherrylakepublishing.com

Content Adviser: Gail Dickinson, PhD, Associate Professor, Old Dominion University

Book design and illustration: The Design Lab

Photo credits: Cover, ©Yuri Arcurs/Shutterstock, Inc.; page 5, ©Saskia Massink/
Dreamstime.com; page 8, ©Neale Cousland/Dreamstime.com; page 9, ©Rmarmion/
Dreamstime.com; page 14, ©Noam Armon/Dreamstime.com; page 15, ©Maurie
Hill/Dreamstime.com; page 17, ©Mogens Trolle/Shutterstock, Inc.; page 19, ©Ewan
Chesser/Shutterstock, Inc.

Library of Congress Cataloging-in-Publication Data
Truesdell, Ann.
 Find the facts with encyclopedias/by Ann Truesdell.
    p. cm.—(Information explorer junior)
 Includes bibliographical references and index.
 ISBN 978-1-61080-367-0 (lib. bdg.)—ISBN 978-1-61080-376-2 (e-book.)—
ISBN 978-1-61080-392-2 (pbk.)
1. Encyclopedias and dictionaries—Juvenile literature. I. Title.
 AG5.T78 2012
 031.02—dc23                              2011034504

Cherry Lake Publishing would like to acknowledge
the work of The Partnership for 21st Century Skills.
Please visit *www.21stcenturyskills.org* for more information.

Printed in the United States of America
Corporate Graphics Inc.
January 2012
CLSP10

# Table of Contents

CHAPTER ONE

# What Is an Encyclopedia?

Ribbit!

Have you ever wondered why a frog croaks? Do you know how a plane flies? Has your teacher ever asked you to find information about another country? Do you want to learn more about a person who lived a long time ago? All of this and much more can be found in an **encyclopedia**.

Sometimes, you want to use many sources to find a lot of information. Researchers call this in-depth information. Sometimes, you just want one source that explains something without going in-depth. This is called an **overview**. Encyclopedias are books that contain overviews on many topics.

The overviews in an encyclopedia are called **articles**. Each article contains the most important facts about a topic. Encyclopedias are a great place to start learning about a topic that is new to you.

Encyclopedias contain information on a wide variety of topics.

Most encyclopedias have information about every important topic that you can think of. Articles on people, places, events, and things can be found there. Other encyclopedias are about only one subject. An example is an animal encyclopedia. There, you find articles only about different types of animals. Many times, an encyclopedia tells you other places where you can find more information.

Each article in an encyclopedia is written by an **expert** on the topic. An expert is a person who knows a lot about a subject. Another person checks the facts in the article to make sure that they are correct. It takes a lot of people to write an encyclopedia.

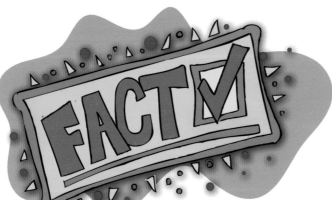

Fact checkers make sure the information in encyclopedias is reliable.

Wikis can be helpful, but they don't always have reliable information.

One popular online encyclopedia is Wikipedia. Wikipedia is a type of Web site called a **wiki**. On a wiki, anyone can write part of the article. Some of these people might be experts on the topic. Others might not, so the information they write may not be correct. It's best to double-check the information you get from a wiki. You want to be sure that what you are reading is a fact.

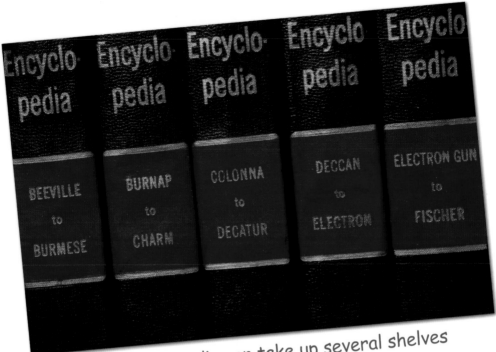

A printed encyclopedia can take up several shelves at a library.

Some encyclopedias are printed sets of books. Other encyclopedias are on the Internet. An online encyclopedia may look like a Web site. But encyclopedias are very different from normal books or Web sites. You can learn basic information about your topic from an encyclopedia. Then, you can check out a book or a Web site if you need more details.

To get a copy of this activity, visit www.cherrylakepublishing.com/activities.

# Activity

You can usually find printed encyclopedias in your classroom, school library, or public library. There are many online encyclopedias. Some are free only if you visit them from your school or public library, or with a password at home. Explore each kind of encyclopedia you find. Try to find one that is made for kids. Look for another that only has information about animals. Each kind of encyclopedia is useful for different reasons.

Librarians or teachers can show you how to access online encyclopedias at school.

CHAPTER TWO

# Finding the Article You Need

Now it's time to look up information about your topic. How do you start? It depends on what kind of encyclopedia you are using.

Printed encyclopedias organize information in different ways. Large encyclopedias are made up of a set of books. There might be a book for each letter of the alphabet. Each individual book in the set is called a **volume**. You have to find the correct volume that covers your topic.

Let's say you are **researching** apples. Look for the volume that begins with the letter "A." It contains all the topics that start with "A." Open up that volume and look for the word "apples." It will appear in alphabetical order. It's just like using a dictionary.

It may also help to check the **index** of the encyclopedia. An encyclopedia index is a separate volume. It lists all of the topics in every volume of the encyclopedia. It tells you which volume to use to find your topic. For example, look up "panther" in the index. You will find that the article about this large cat is under the subject heading "cougar."

Cougars and panthers are the same kind of animal.

The index might also help you find information contained in another article. For example, information about pandas might be in the "P" volume. But it might also be found in the "C" volume, under "China." That's because pandas come from China.

You can learn more about pandas by researching China.

Some encyclopedias only have information about certain topics.

Not all printed encyclopedias are made up of many volumes. Encyclopedias about animals, countries, or the human body might only be one volume. Topics are listed in alphabetical order. You can also find information in the index.

If you are using an online encyclopedia, you will find your topic in a different way. You usually search for your topic by typing the word into a search box. Make sure to spell your topic correctly. If you do not, your search may have no results.

Keep your search terms simple. Let's say you want to know who invented the automobile. You should not type in "Who invented the car?" Instead, think about what subject heading you would look up in a print encyclopedia. Try using the words

Choose your search words carefully.

Cars are just one of the many subjects you can learn about by using an encyclopedia.

"automobile" or "car" in your search. Then read the article to see if you can learn about the first car and who invented it. You might need to narrow your search. Use terms such as "invented automobile" or "invented car" or "inventor of the automobile." Are your search results better? Read those articles to see if you can find the information you're looking for.

# Activity

Searching for an article in a printed encyclopedia is different from searching in an online encyclopedia. What is the best way to search for a subject in both types of encyclopedias? Look at the questions below. Let's come up with some ideas for how to search for answers.

### How often does a lion hunt?

Look for "Lion" in a printed encyclopedia. It might be in the "L" volume of a large encyclopedia. Or it might be found in a single encyclopedia of animals. Online, "lion" might be your best search term. The term "lion hunting" might give you results about people who hunt for lions. The search terms "hunt" and "hunting" will give you articles on all types of hunting. It might even give you articles on people or animals that hunt.

Try using an encyclopedia to learn all you can about how lions hunt for food.

### Does it get cold in Brazil?

"Brazil" should be your search term in a printed encyclopedia. You should find an article about the country. Information about the country's weather will be in that article. Online, narrowing your search will make it easier to find the information you need. Type in terms such as "Brazil weather" or "Brazil climate."

To get a copy of this activity, visit www.cherrylakepublishing.com/activities.

# CHAPTER THREE

# Exploring the Article

Each encyclopedia article has lots of information. You may need to read the entire article to find out what you want to know. Large articles may be divided into themes with subheadings. Subheadings are like small headlines.

You can quickly **skim** the subheadings. That means you are reading them just to find the information you want. The article may have pictures, maps, or timelines with it. An online encyclopedia may also have videos and links to other resources.

Look for important words in the article that relate to your topic. Let's say you want to know what a panther eats. Find an encyclopedia article about panthers. Then skim the article for words such as "diet," "food," "prey," or "hunt." Searching for important words on the page of an online encyclopedia is easy. Go to your browser's "find" feature. (Try pressing the Ctrl and F keys or the Command and F keys). Then type in one of those words. It will bring you right to the spot in the article that has that information.

What did you learn about panthers?

# Activity

Sometimes encyclopedia articles have more information than you need. Then it's time to skim the article. Let's use the same topics from the last activity for this activity. Find an article on each of these topics. Now think of some important words to look for. Skim the article and try to find them.

### How often does a lion hunt?

Look for sections or paragraphs containing the words "hunting," "prey," "predator," "stalk," or "food." You might even see a picture of a lion on the prowl. That could mean the information you're looking for is close by.

### Does it get cold in Brazil?

Skip to a section or paragraph about "climate," "weather," or "temperature." Then read the information to see what the weather is like during different seasons.

Encyclopedias can teach you a lot about geography, history, and science. But encyclopedias cover more topics than just those you learn in school. There are print and online encyclopedias that cover lots of unusual and interesting subjects. There are encyclopedias of magical spells, comic book superheroes, vampires and monsters, and card tricks. There's even an encyclopedia of sandwiches! What are you interested in? A print or online encyclopedia can probably teach you a lot more about it!

# Glossary

**articles (AR-ti-kuhlz)** summaries of information about different topics, which are found in an encyclopedia

**encyclopedia (en-sye-kloh-PEE-dee-uh)** a book or set of books with information about many different subjects

**expert (EK-spurt)** someone who is very skilled at something or knows a lot about a particular subject

**index (IN-deks)** a separate volume of an encyclopedia that lists all of the topics the encyclopedia covers

**researching (REE-surch-ing)** looking for more information on a topic

**overview (OH-vur-vue)** a general summary of information that quickly explains a lot without going in-depth

**skim (SKIM)** to read through something quickly, just to get the main ideas

**volume (VOL-yuhm)** one book within a set of books; printed encyclopedias are often made up of many volumes

**wiki (WIH-kee)** a Web site that allows anyone to add, remove, or change information on it

# Find Out More

## BOOKS

*The New Children's Encyclopedia.* New York: DK Publishing, 2009.

*Scholastic Children's Encyclopedia.* New York: Scholastic
Reference, 2004.

## WEB SITES

**eHow—How to Use an Encyclopedia**

*www.ehow.com/how_2082900_use-encyclopedia.html*
Here's a useful Web site that offers instructions on using an
encyclopedia.

**Helium—How to Use an Encyclopedia**

*www.helium.com/items/2057673-how-to-use-an-encyclopedia*
This site provides easy-to-follow tips on how to get the most out of
your encyclopedia research.

# Index

## About the Author

Ann Truesdell is a school library media specialist and teacher in Michigan. She and her husband, Mike, love traveling and spending time with their children, James and Charlotte.